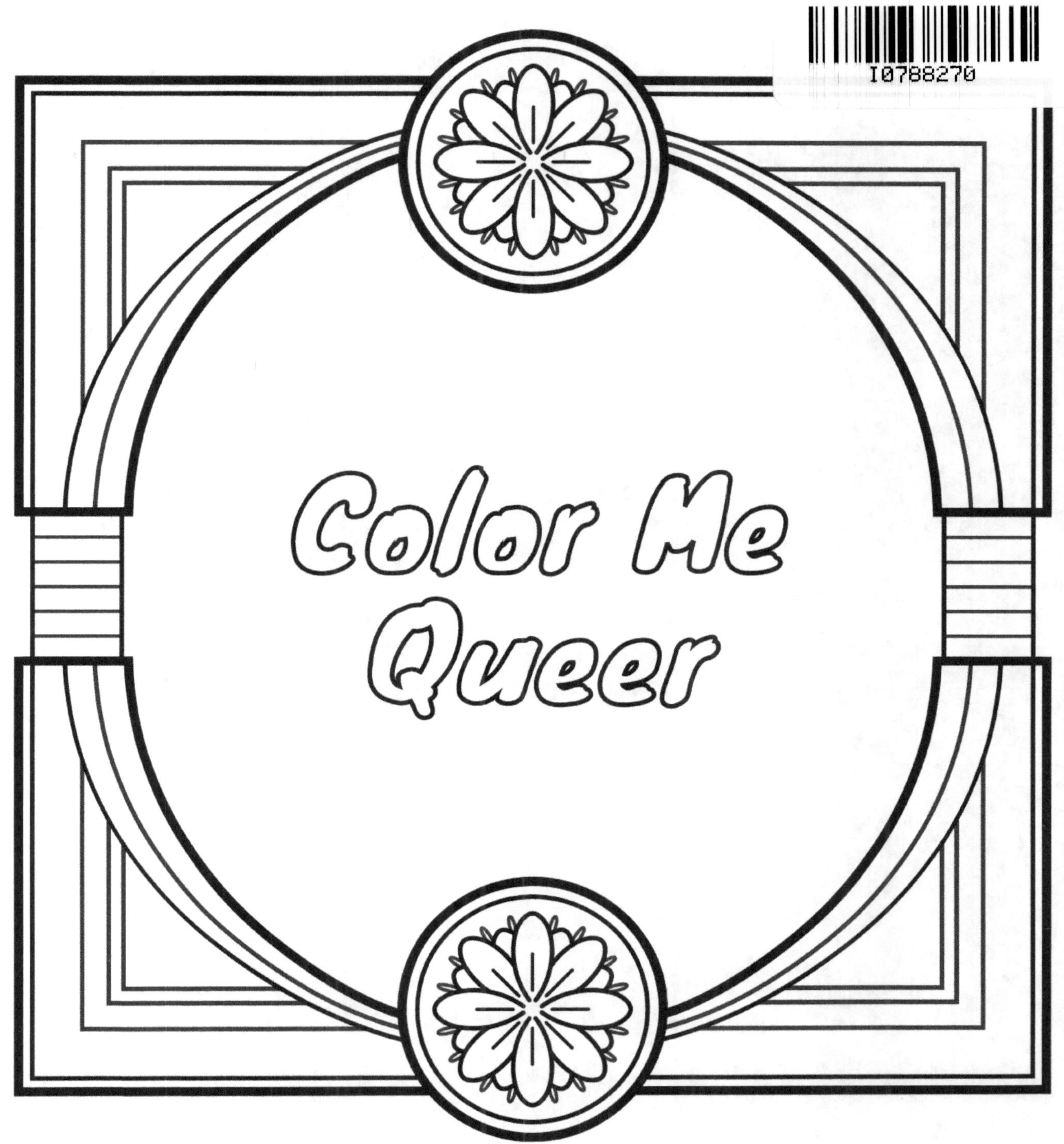

Adult Coloring Book
From The Pride & Joy Foundation

PRIDE & JOY
publishing

An Imprint for GracePoint Publishing (www.GracePointPublishing.com)

GracePoint Matrix, LLC
624 S. Cascade Ave
Suite 201
Colorado Springs, CO 80903
www.GracePointMatrix.com
Email: Admin@GracePointMatrix.com

SAN # 991-6032

A Library of Congress Control Number has been requested and is pending.

ISBN: (Paperback) 978-1-955272-31-5

Books may be purchased for educational, business, or sales promotional use.
For bulk order requests and price schedule contact:
Orders@GracePointPublishing.com

Dear Queer One,

I came out to myself at age 37 and after 17 years of marriage. It took me so long to wrap my head around who I truly was versus who the world wanted me to be. My eyes finally opened to the fact that not only was I queer, but I had a huge queer family that was waiting for me as well. Maybe because I'm an investigator by nature or maybe because I had lost so much community in the coming out process, I became obsessed with learning about my new LGBTQ+ culture and history.

Until that time, I had literally never heard of Harvey Milk or Marsha P. Johnson, let alone Hayley Kiyoko. As new and naive as I felt as a baby gay, my research showed me that I wasn't actually stumbling down a dirt road trying to find my way in the dark. Thousands of people have gone before me: breaking down barriers, changing laws and minds, saying the words I needed to hear.

LGBTQ+ people are some of the few marginalized populations born to families, not of the same marginalized population. Rarely do our parents innately know our culture, our vocabulary, or the tricks to finding success and staying out of trouble. Therefore we often grow up without that guiding light, the touchstone that says "Who I am is exactly who I'm supposed to be."

I hope you find a touchstone or two in this book. I hope that you find quiet moments to color and contemplate the beauty that is exactly who you are. Share your work and thoughts with us using #colormequeer, we'd love to feature you!

In those moments of stumbling in the dark, know that your community is here for you. We were all baby gays at some point, regardless of our biological age. And someday, you will be called on to be that light, that touchstone, for someone else. Be ready.

Our paved roads have no need for gates.

Much love,
Elena Joy, founder
Pride & Joy Foundation

LOVE IS NEVER WRONG.

Melissa Etheridge

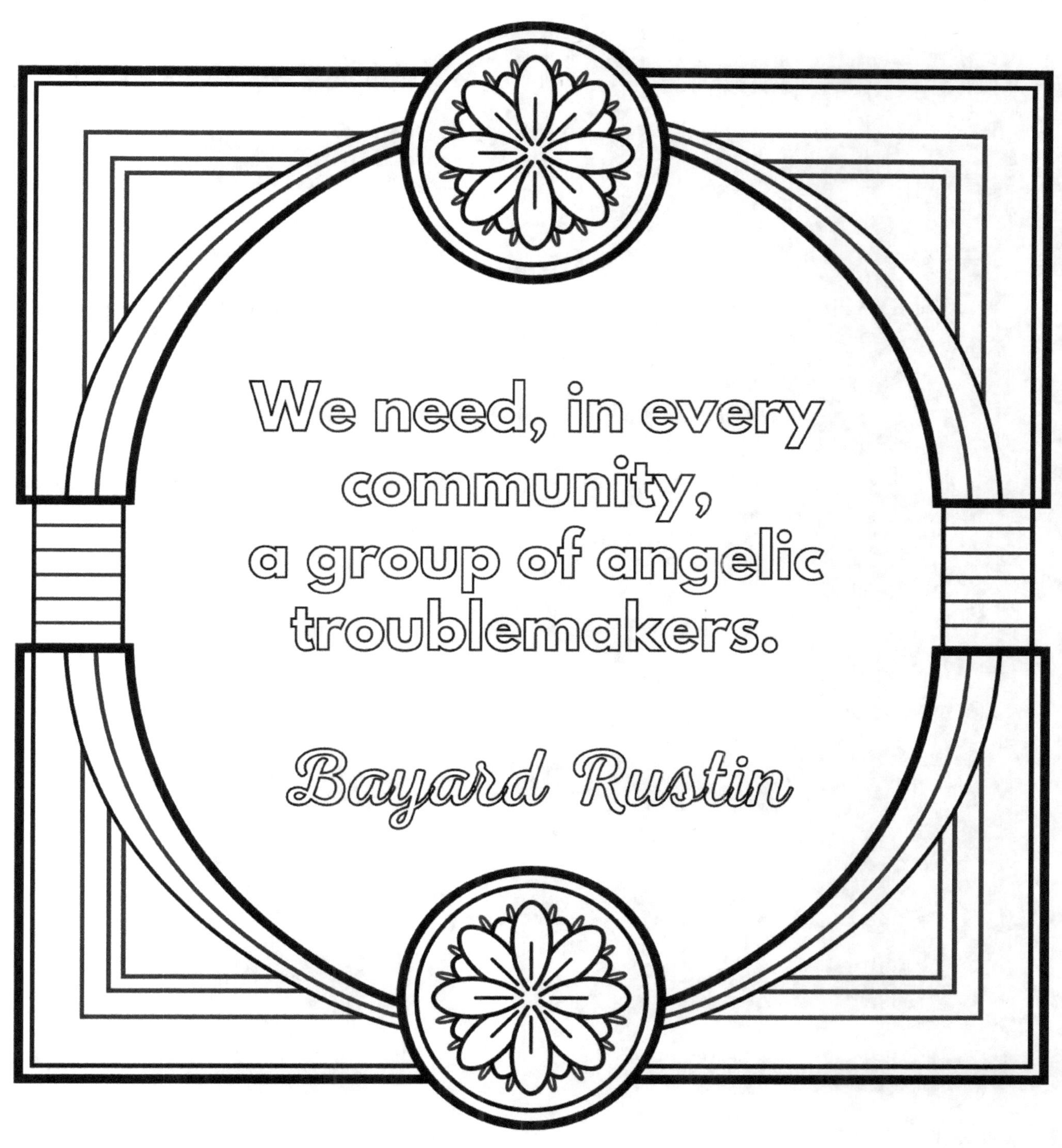

We need, in every
community,
a group of angelic
troublemakers.

Bayard Rustin

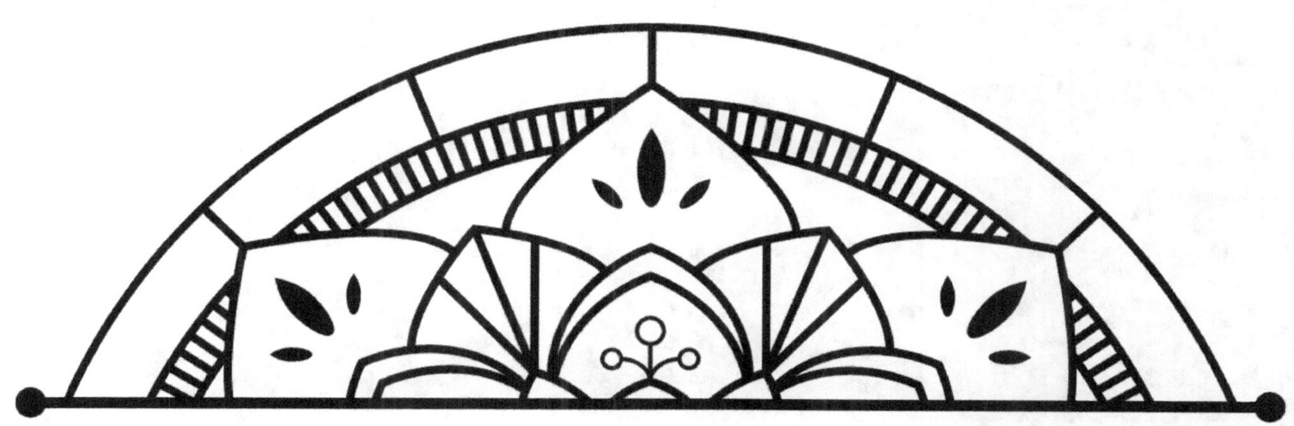

WE CAN DO HARD THINGS.

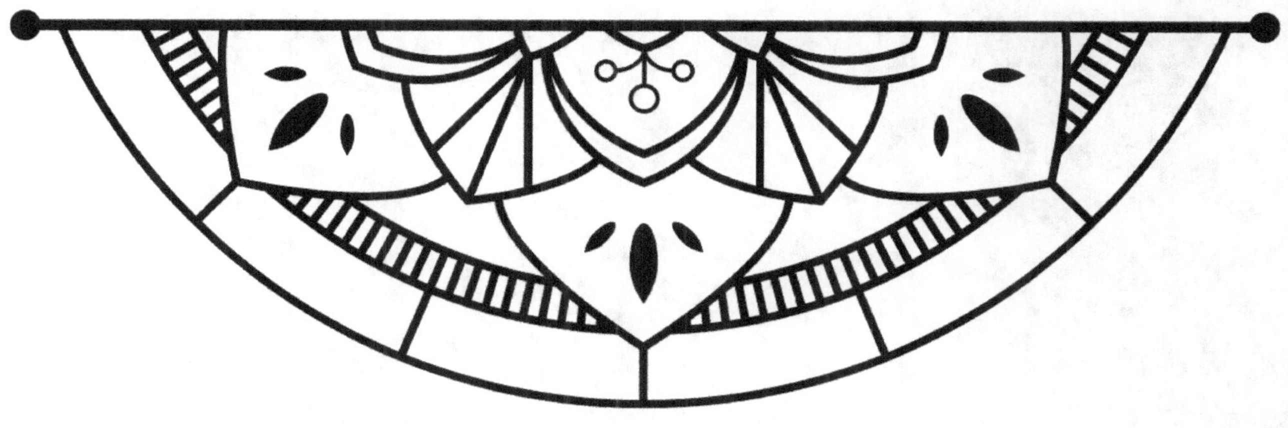

Glennon Doyle

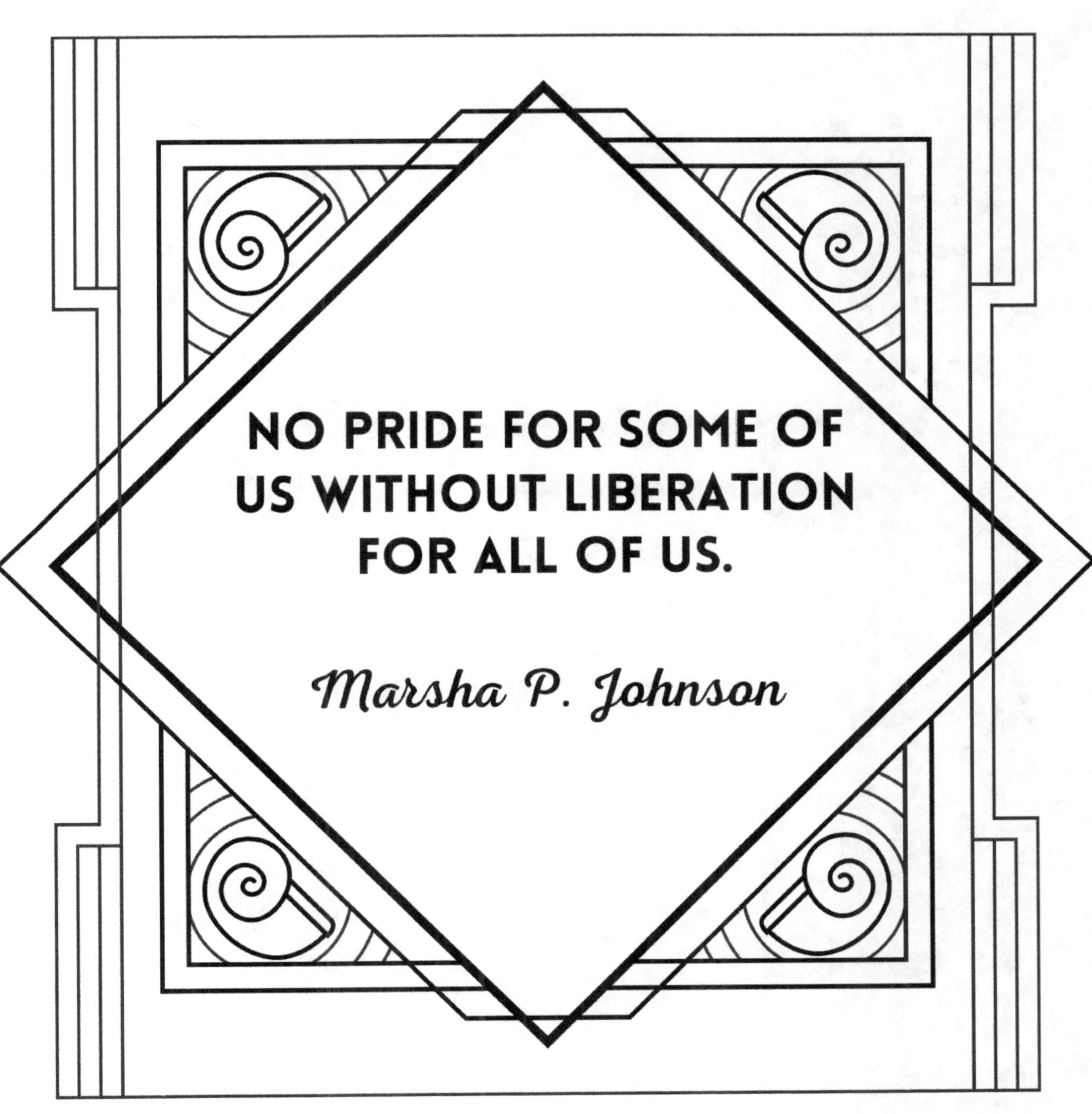

NO PRIDE FOR SOME OF US WITHOUT LIBERATION FOR ALL OF US.

Marsha P. Johnson

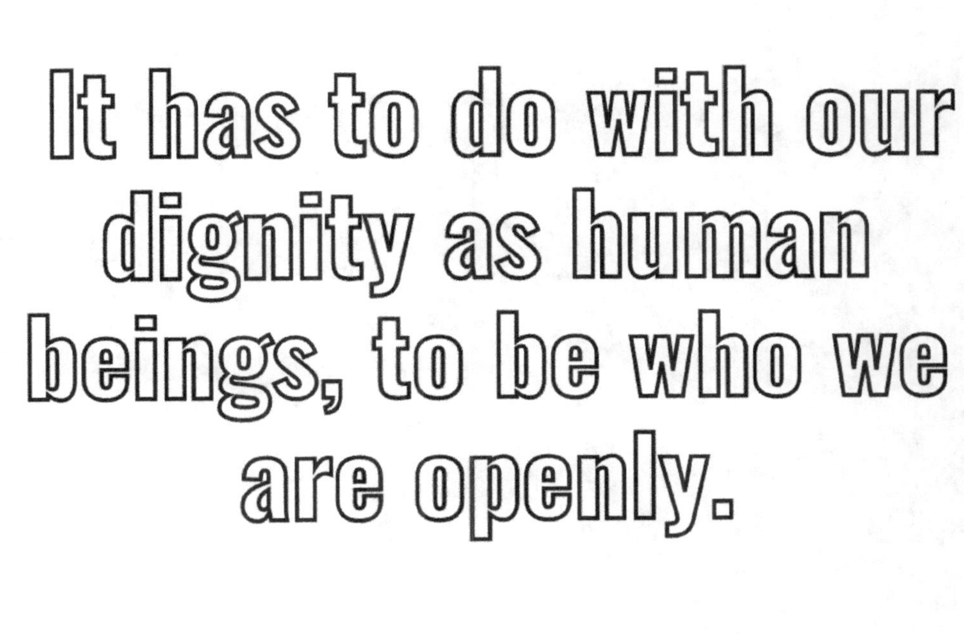
It has to do with our dignity as human beings, to be who we are openly.
Edie Windsor

when we protect the most vulnerable of us, we protect us all.

Elena Joy Thurston

I'M NOT MISSING A MINUTE OF THIS. IT'S THE REVOLUTION!

Sylvia Rivera

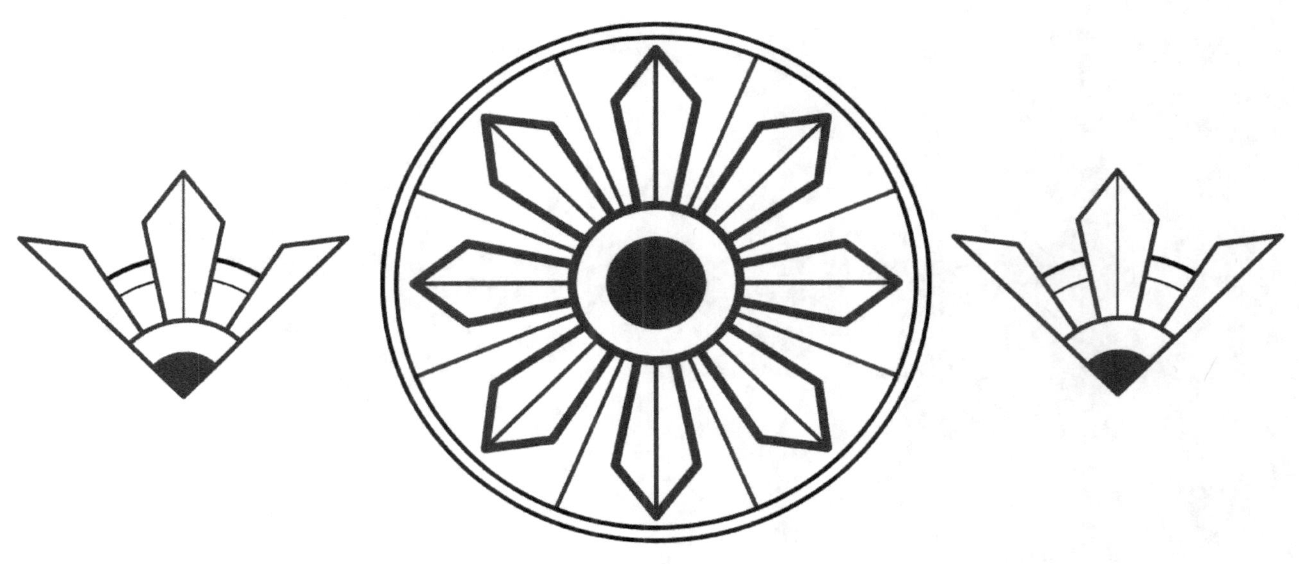

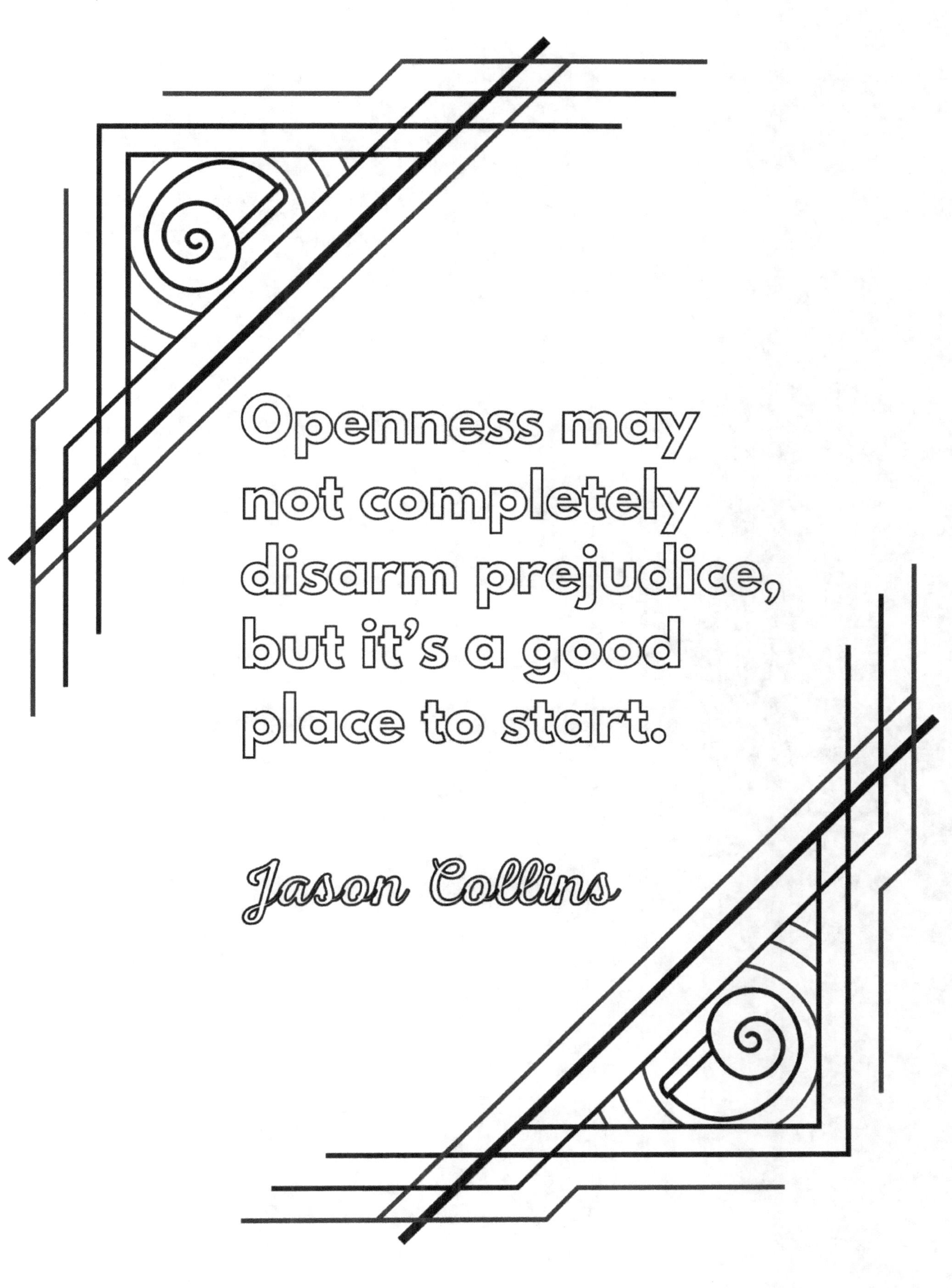
Openness may
not completely
disarm prejudice,
but it's a good
place to start.

Jason Collins

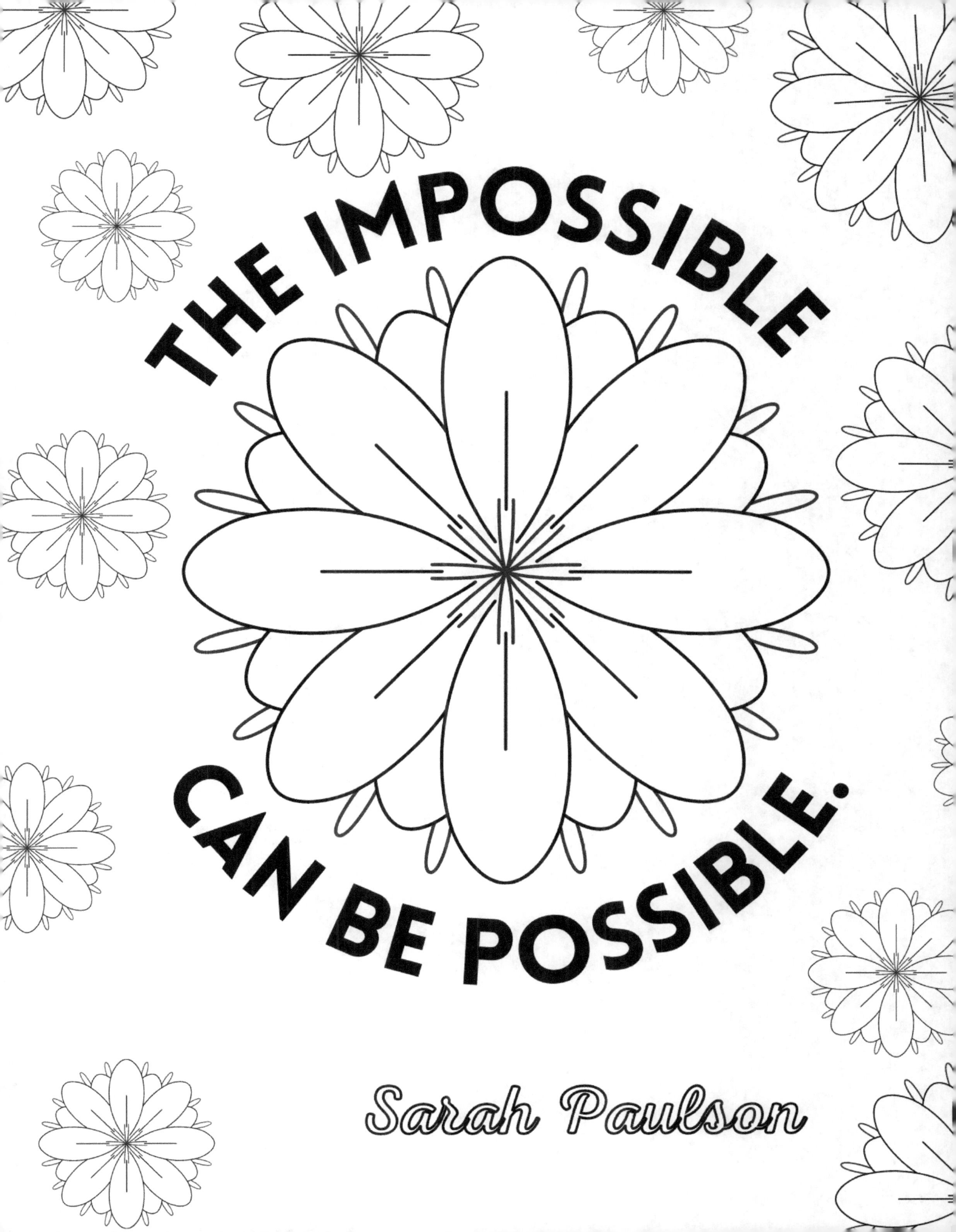

THE IMPOSSIBLE
CAN BE POSSIBLE.
Sarah Paulson

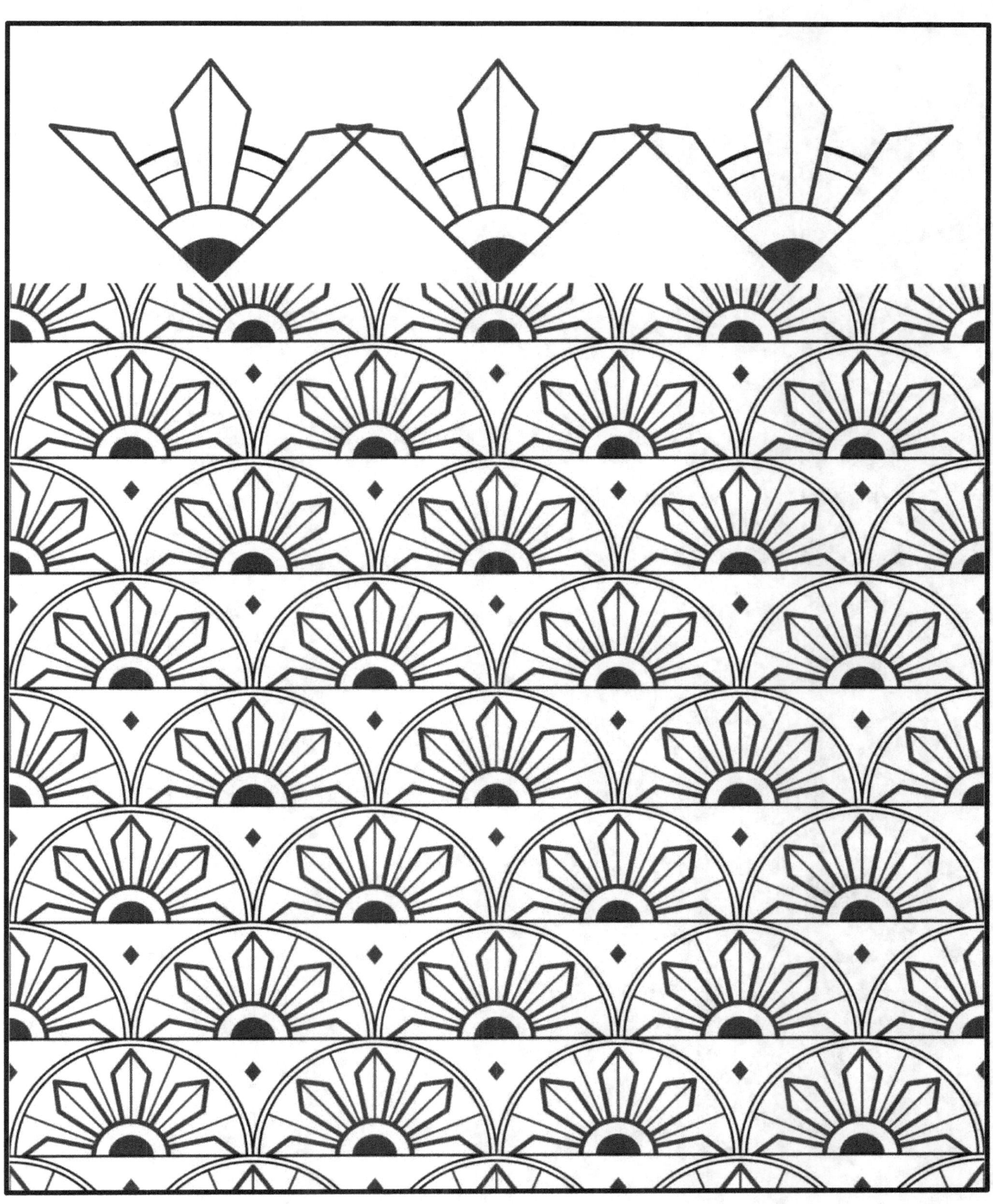

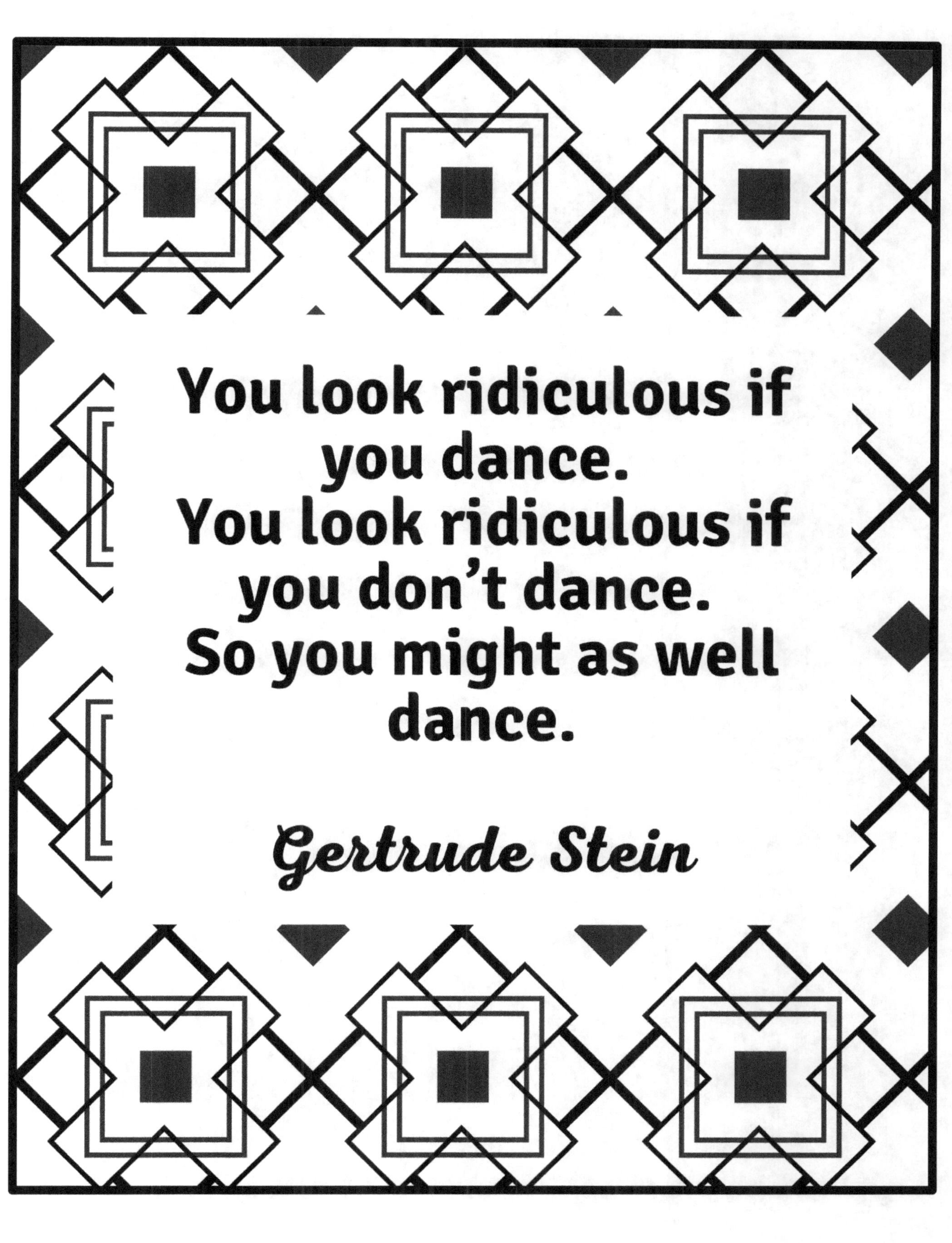

You look ridiculous if you dance.
You look ridiculous if you don't dance.
So you might as well dance.

Gertrude Stein

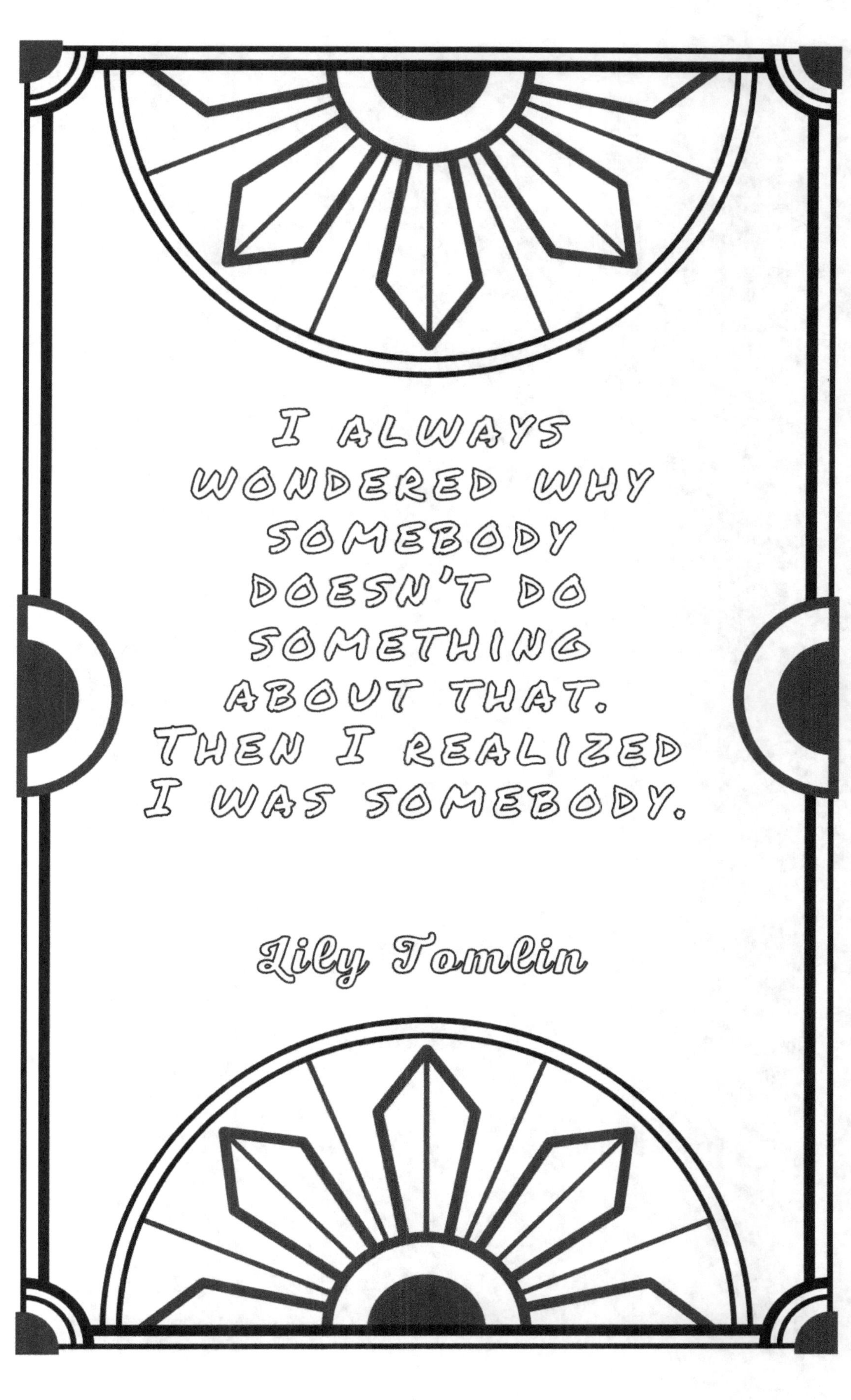
I ALWAYS
WONDERED WHY
SOMEBODY
DOESN'T DO
SOMETHING
ABOUT THAT.
THEN I REALIZED
I WAS SOMEBODY.

Lily Tomlin

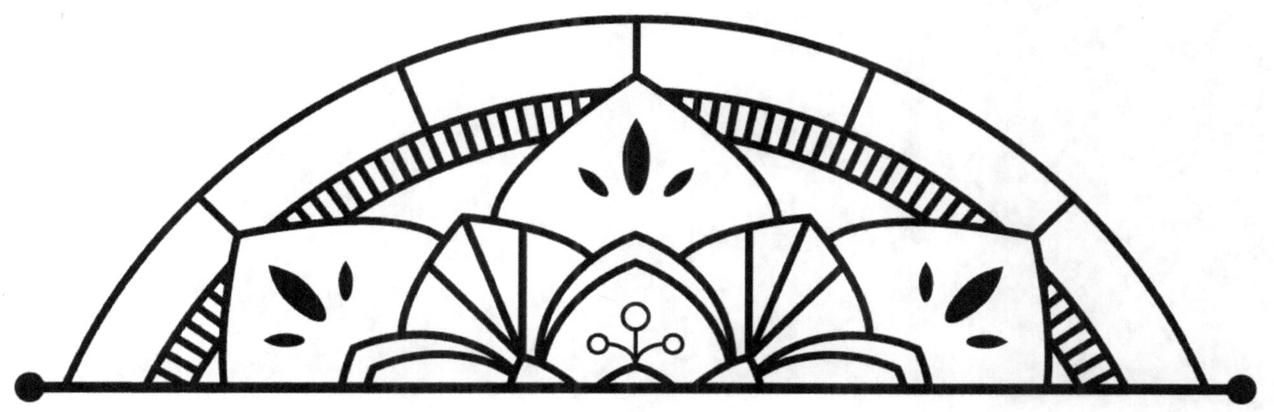

DEFINE YOURSELF.

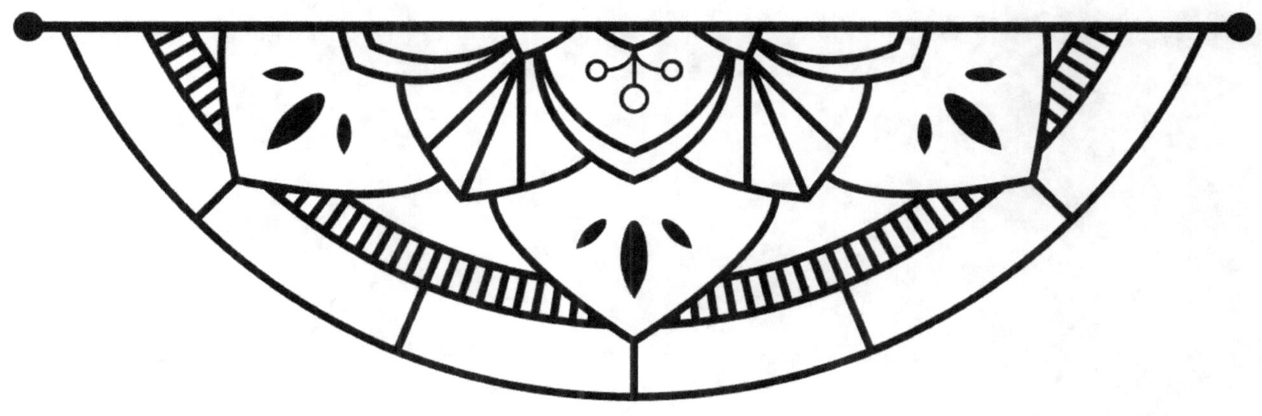

Harvey Fierstein

I've never been
interested in
being invisible
and erased.

Laverne Cox

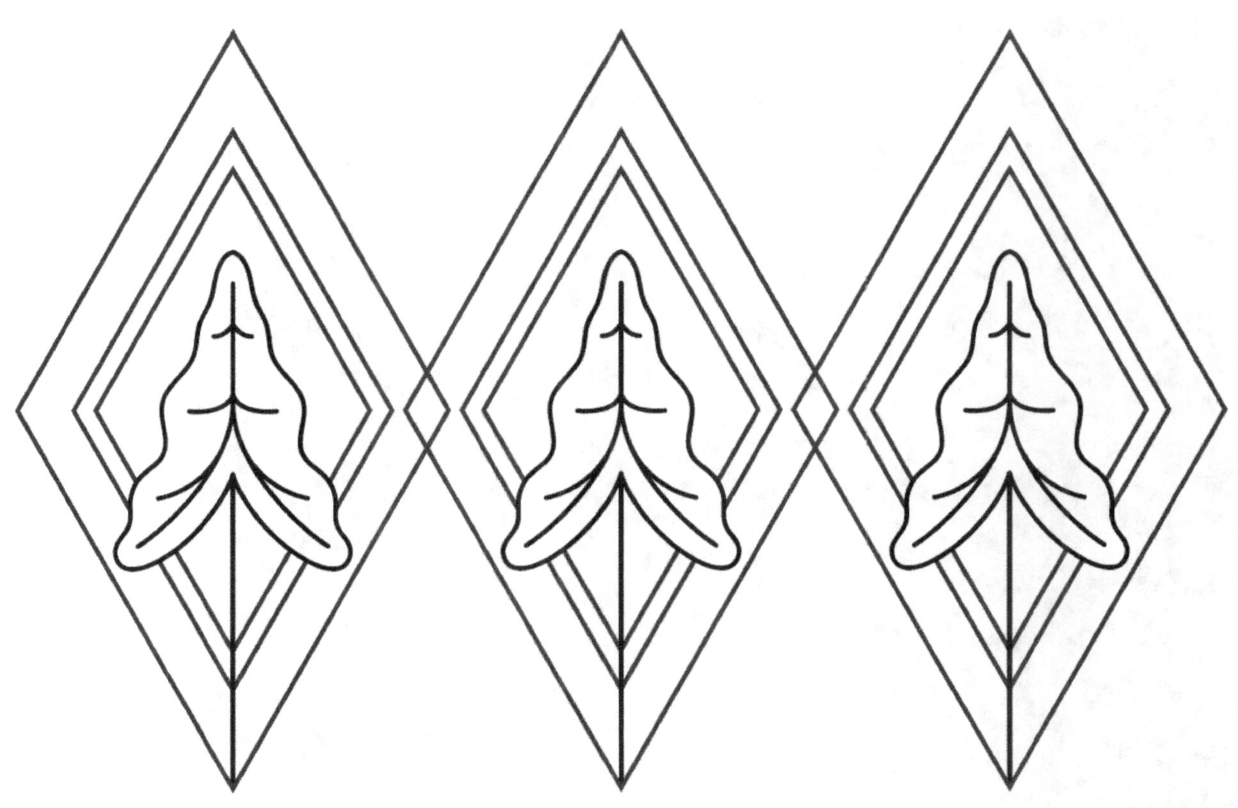

Coming out was one of the most important things I've ever done, lifting from my shoulders the millstone of lies that I hadn't even realized I was carrying.

Sir Ian McKellen

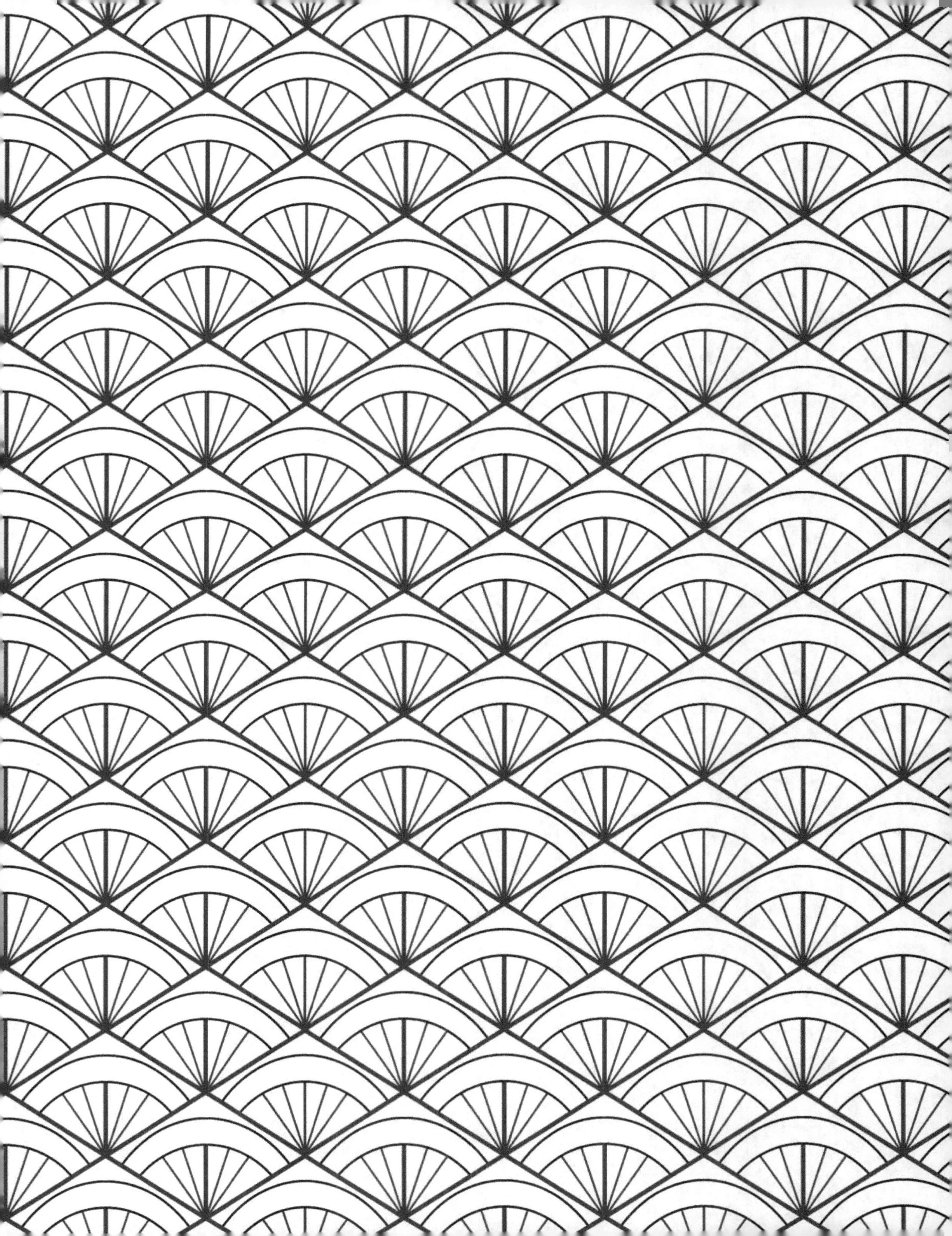

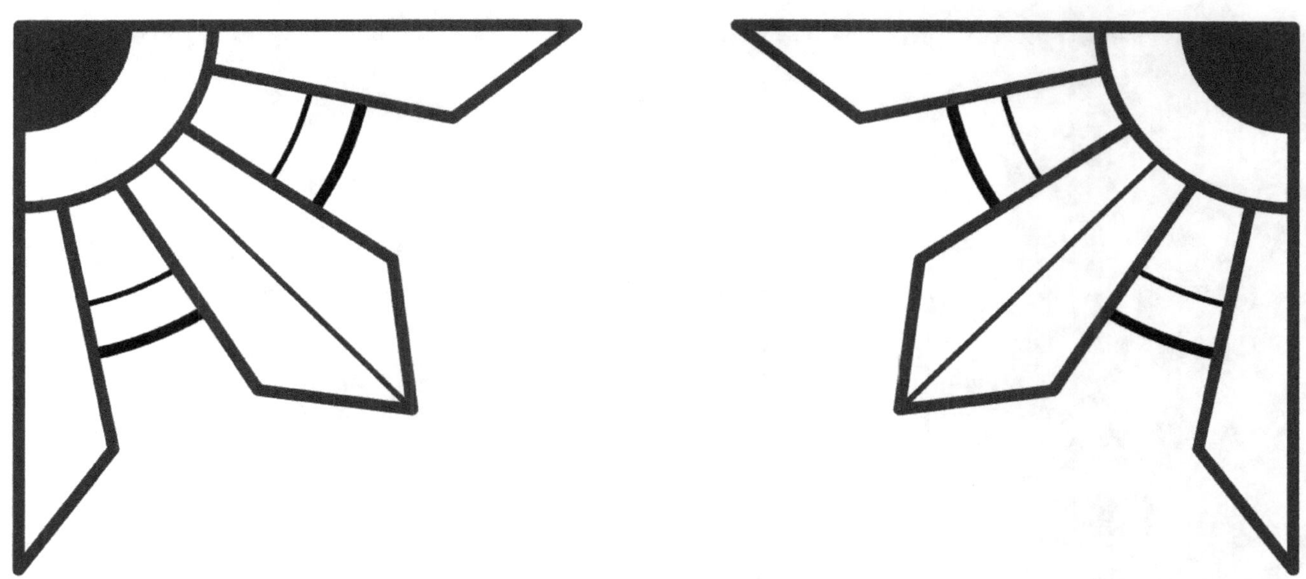

We are powerful because we have survived.

Audre Lorde

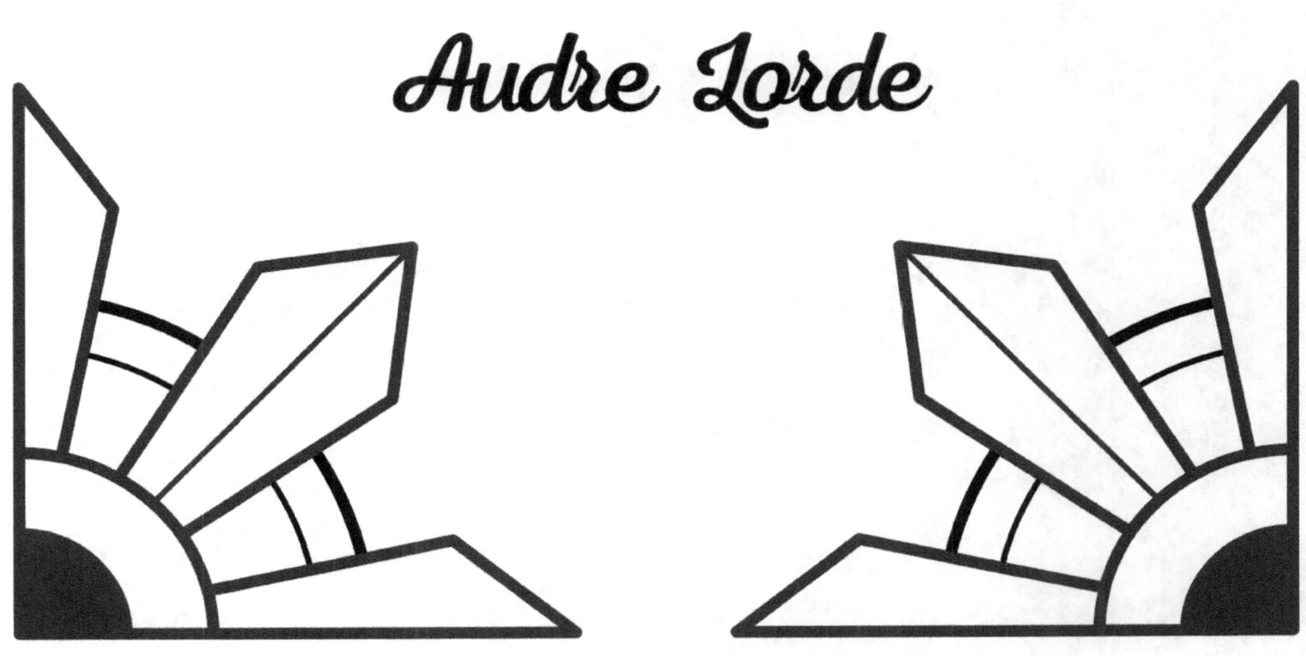

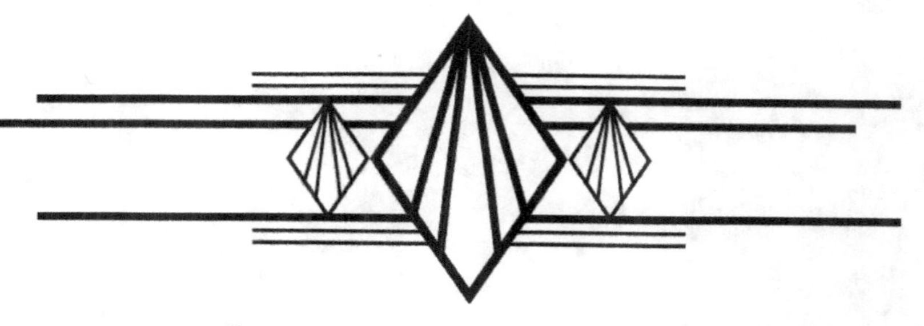
To be yourself is
truly a
revolutionary act

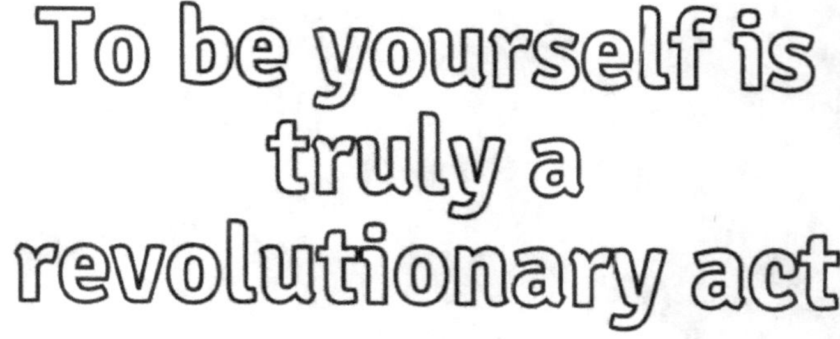
...it's gotten me a
pretty cool life.

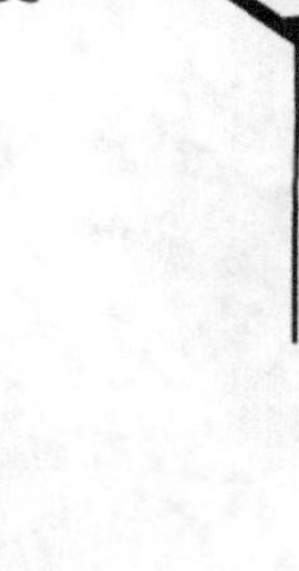

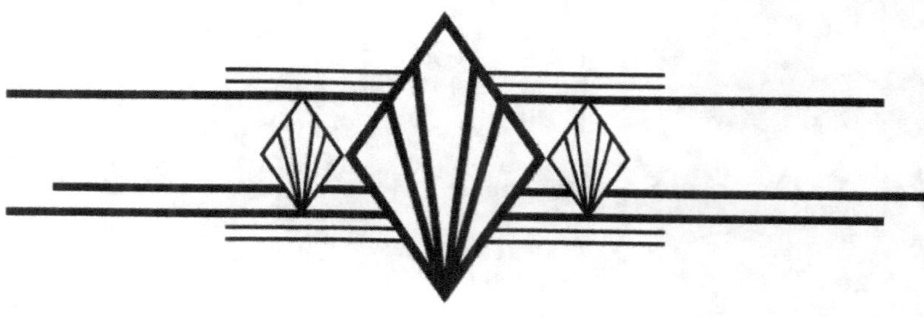
Lena Waithe

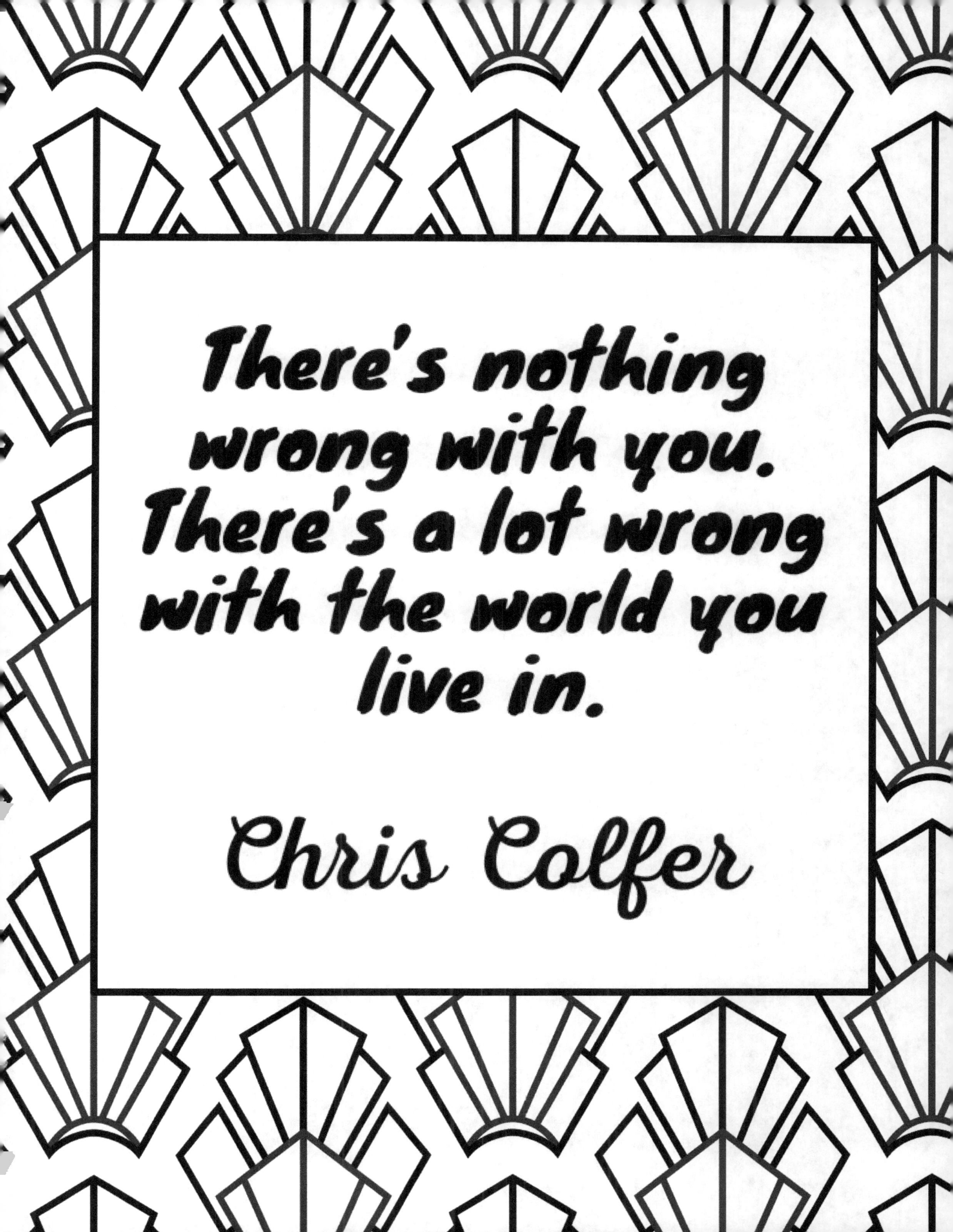

There's nothing wrong with you. There's a lot wrong with the world you live in.

Chris Colfer

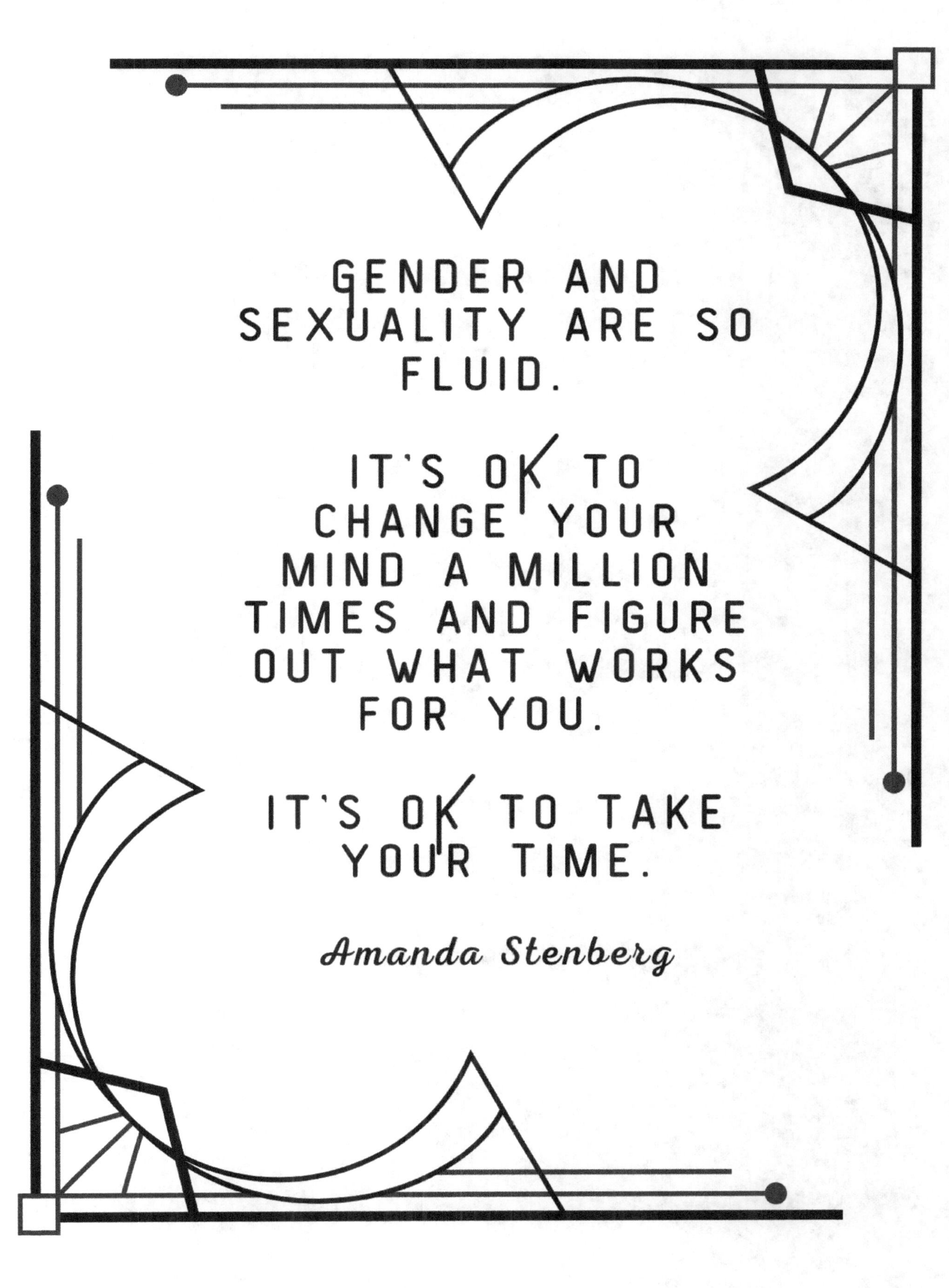

GENDER AND SEXUALITY ARE SO FLUID.

IT'S OK TO CHANGE YOUR MIND A MILLION TIMES AND FIGURE OUT WHAT WORKS FOR YOU.

IT'S OK TO TAKE YOUR TIME.

Amanda Stenberg

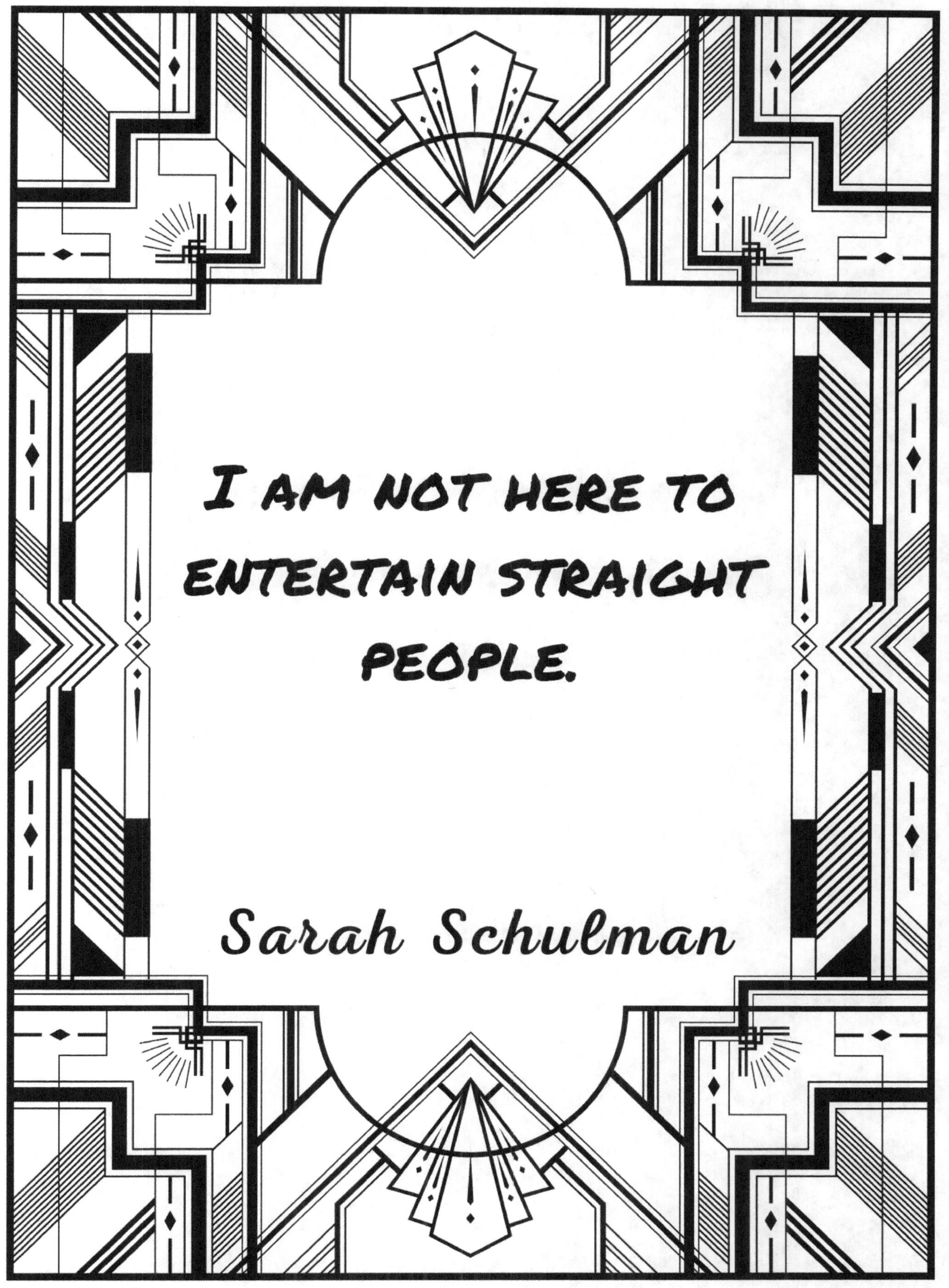

I AM NOT HERE TO ENTERTAIN STRAIGHT PEOPLE.

Sarah Schulman

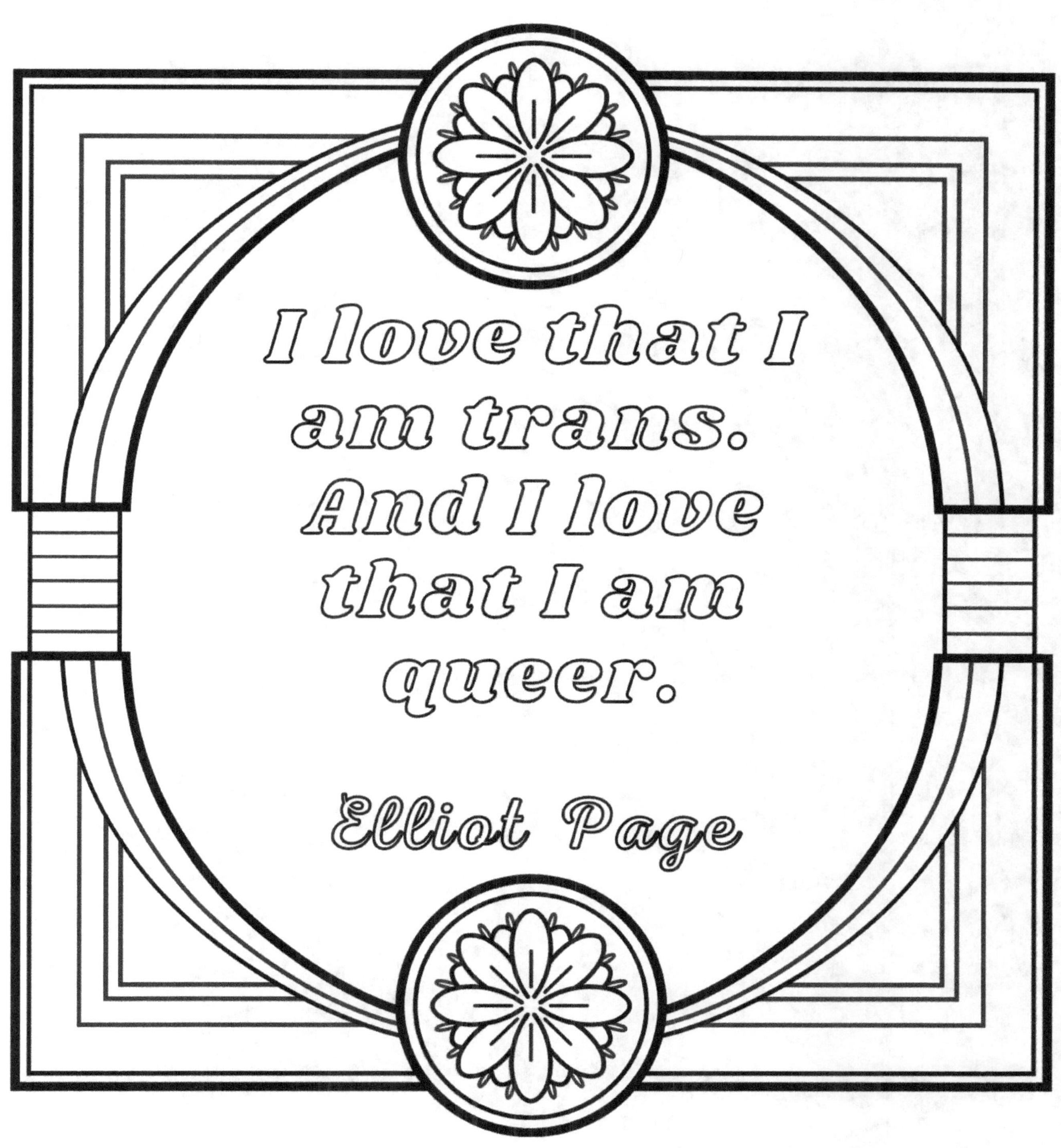

I love that I am trans. And I love that I am queer.
Elliot Page

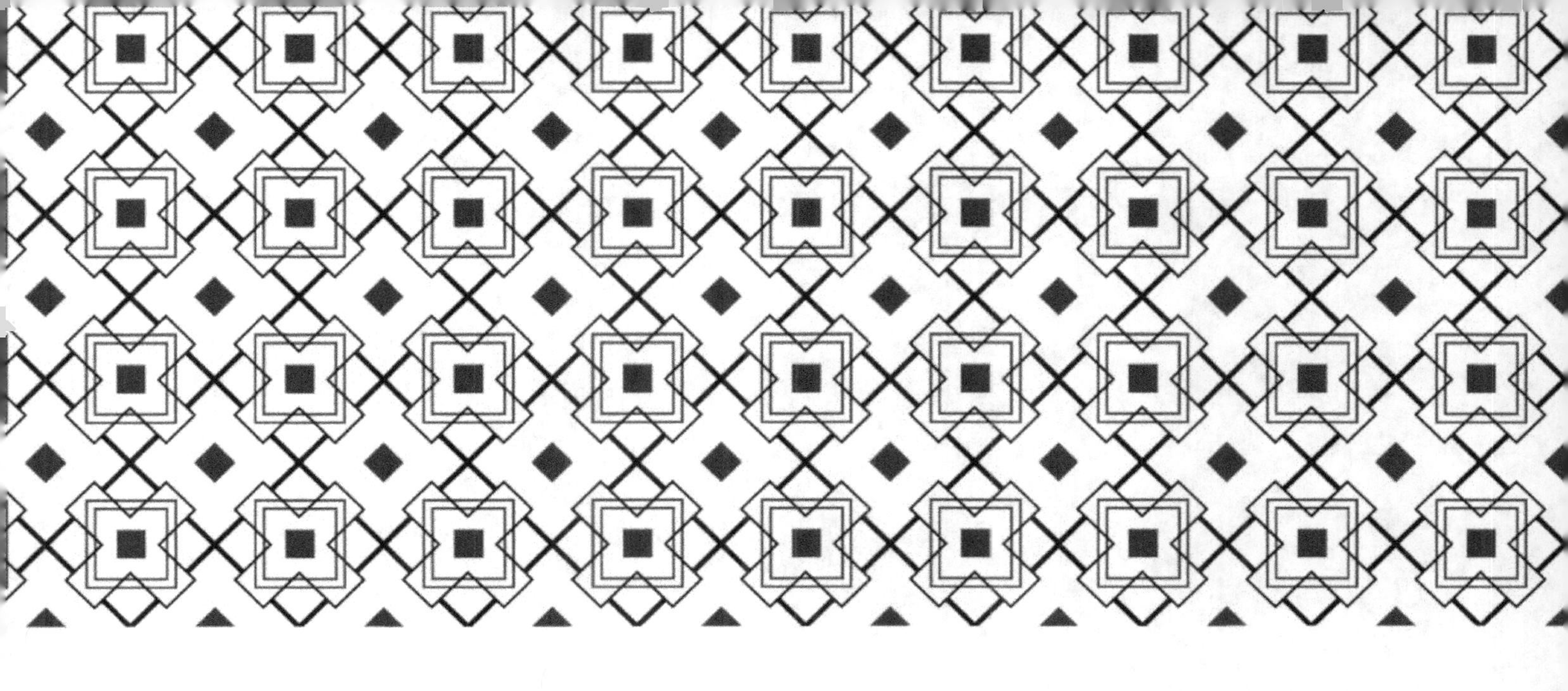

FREEDOM IS TOO ENORMOUS TO BE SLIPPED UNDER A CLOSET DOOR.

Harvey Milk

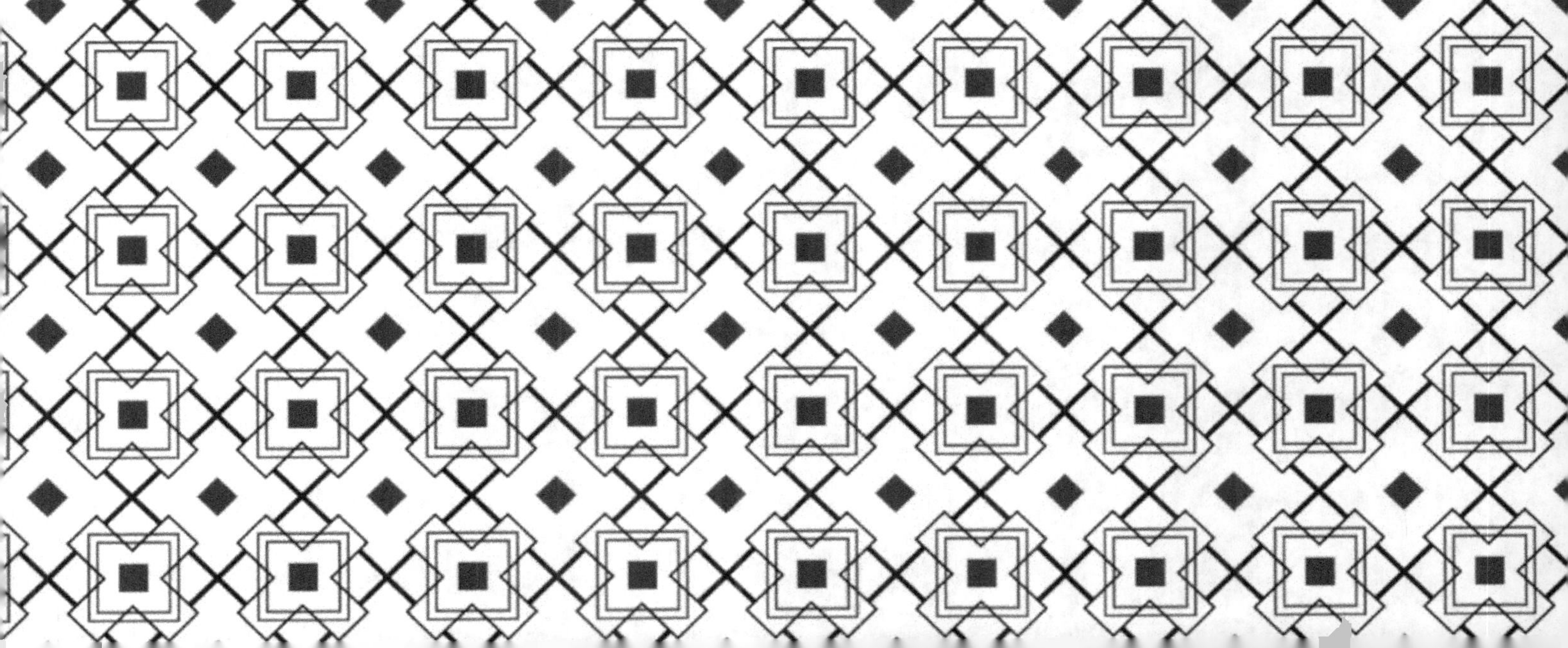

The time for you
to love yourself,
and express
yourself the way
you truly feel,
is now.

Nikkie de Jager

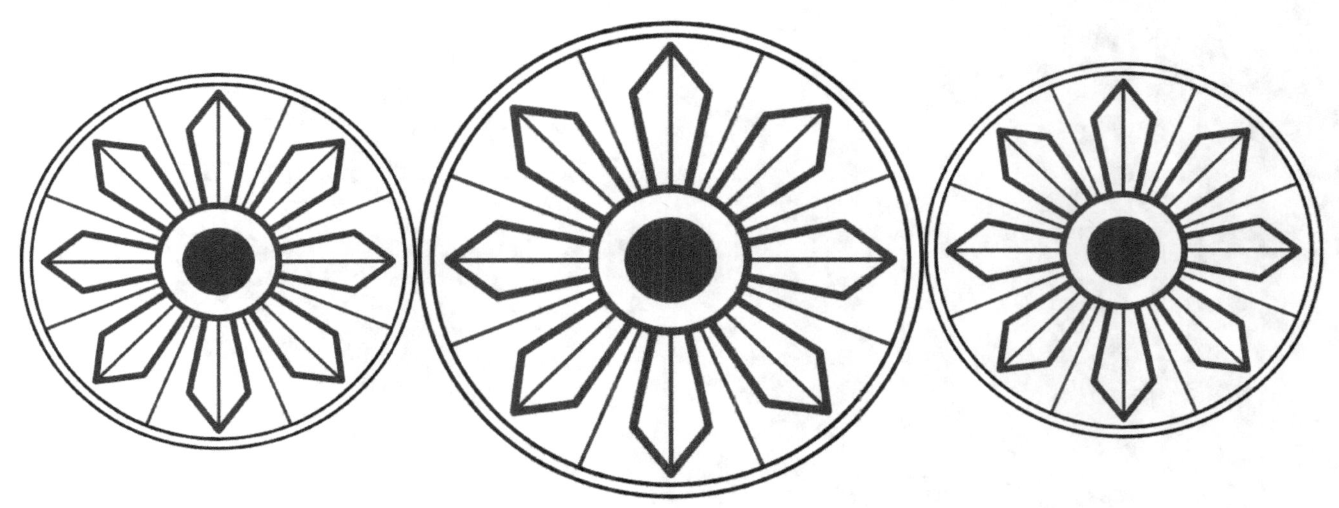

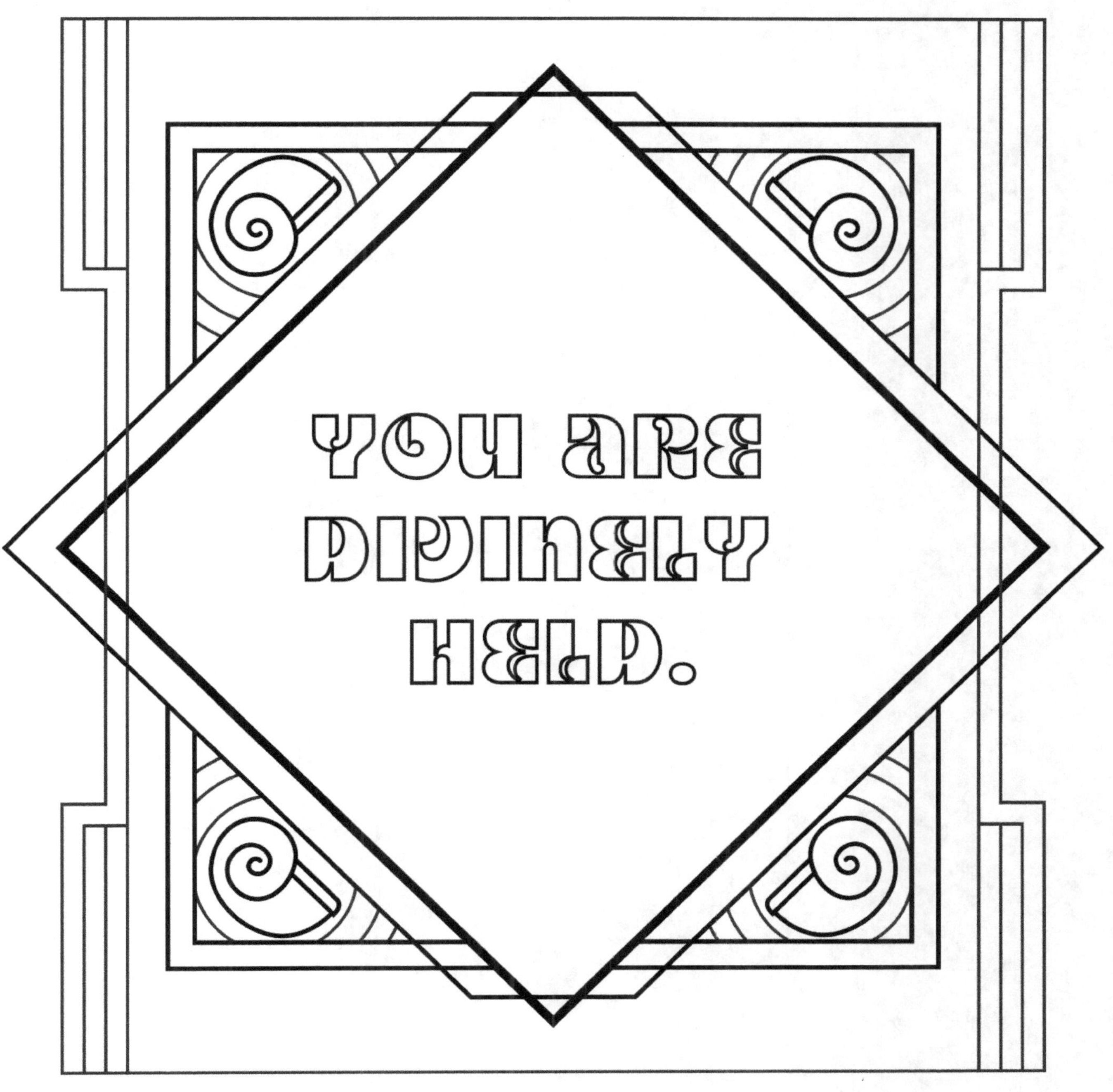

Tommy Dorfman

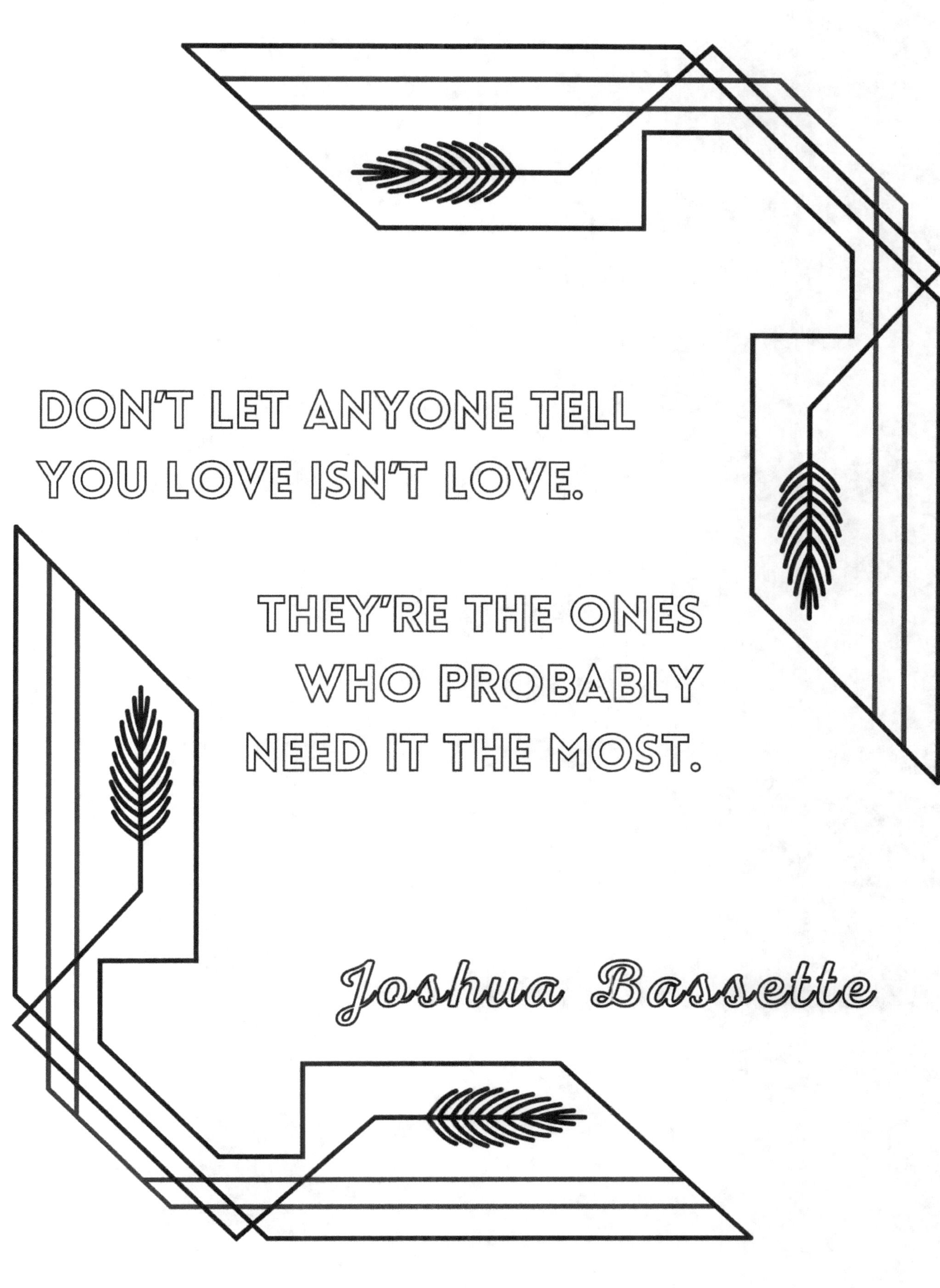
DON'T LET ANYONE TELL YOU LOVE ISN'T LOVE.

THEY'RE THE ONES WHO PROBABLY NEED IT THE MOST.

Joshua Bassette

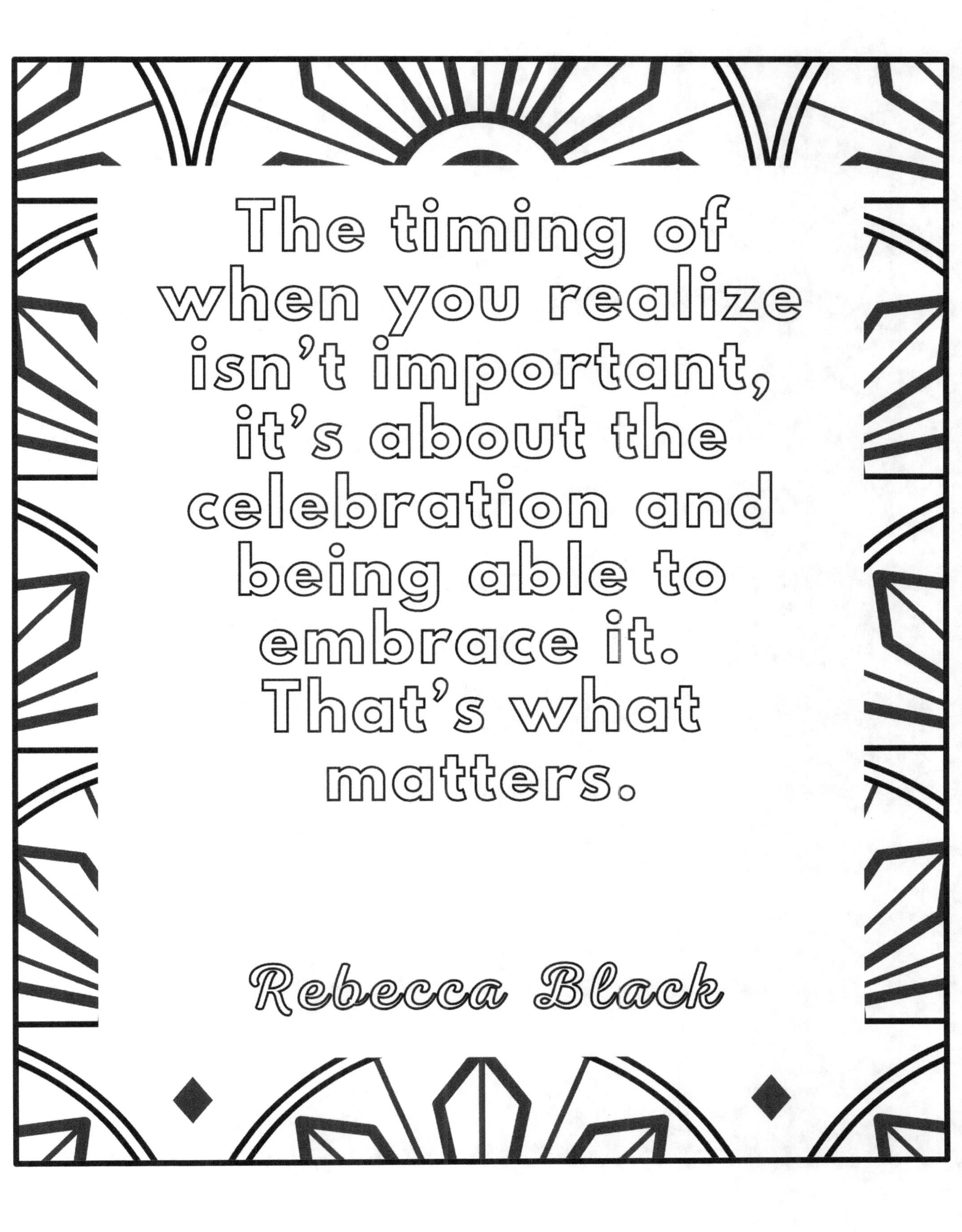

The timing of when you realize isn't important, it's about the celebration and being able to embrace it. That's what matters.

Rebecca Black

I'm here to tell you that not only do you belong, but you are loved and supported.

I see you and I applaud you for just being you.

Billy Porter

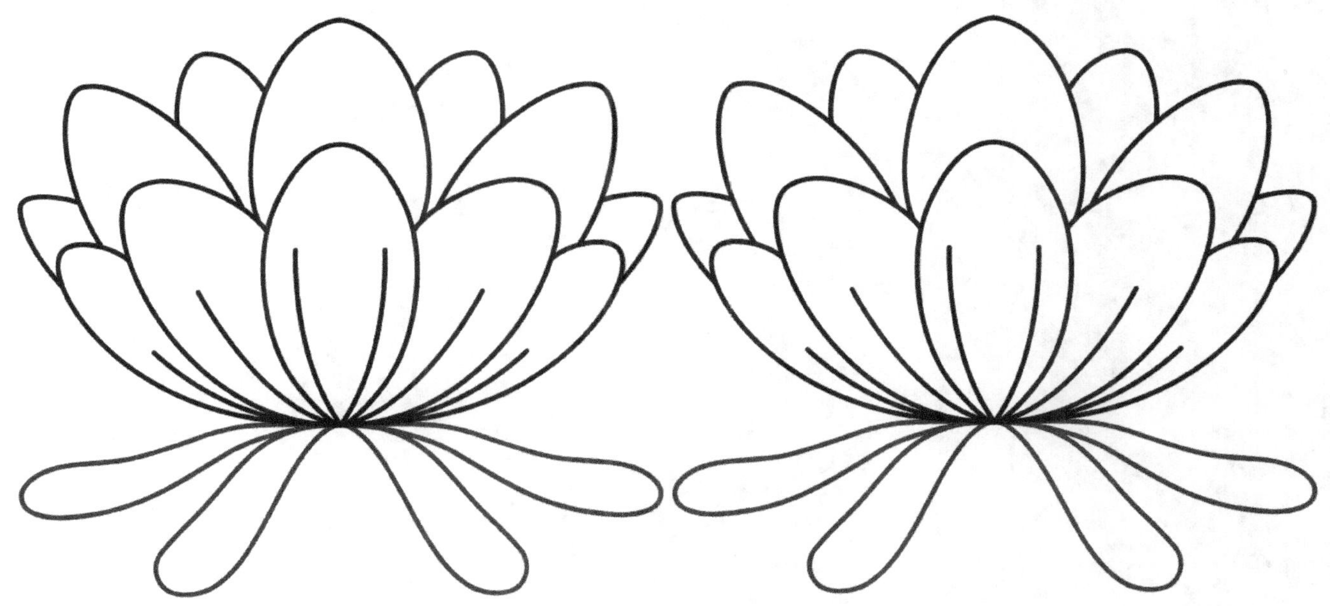

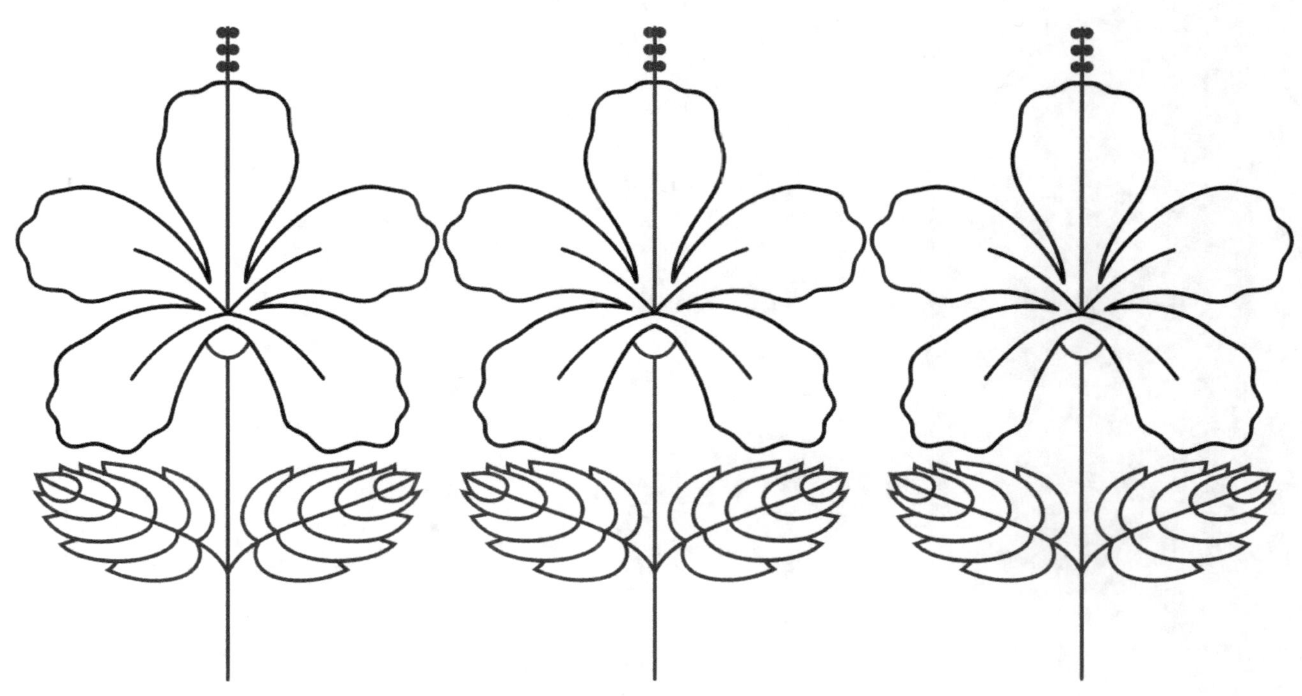

Send your light into the world, and accept all the deserved goodness that comes your way.

Auli'i Cravalho

You are worthy.
You are
powerful.
You will break
barriers.
You will be
challenged.
You will
persevere.

Hayley Kiyoko